50 THINGS YOU REALLY NEED TO KNOW...

YUCKY STUFF

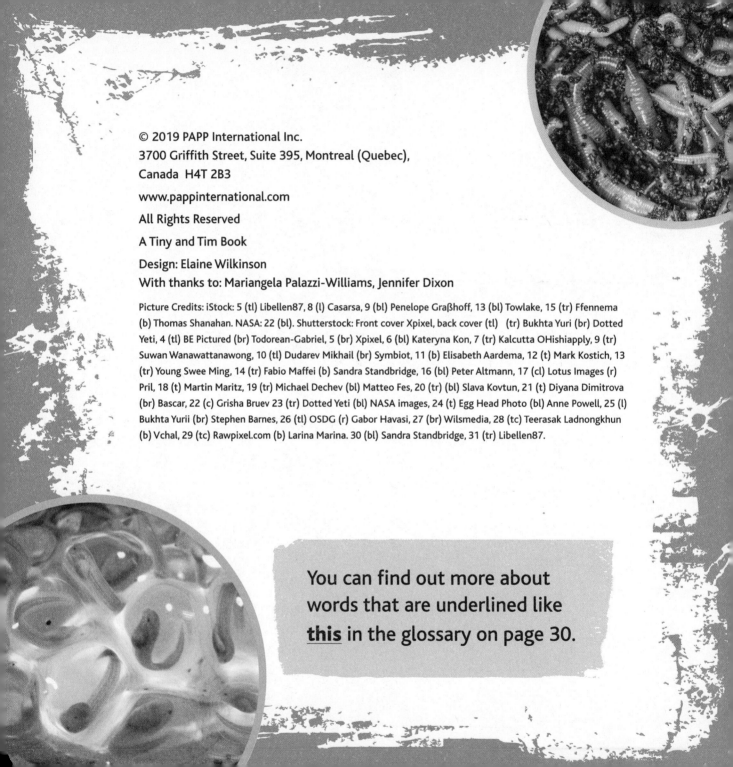

A Tiny and Tim Book

Design: Elaine Wilkinson

With thanks to: Mariangela Palazzi-Williams, Jennifer Dixon

Picture Credits: iStock: 5 (tl) Libellen87, 8 (l) Casarsa, 9 (bl) Penelope Graßhoff, 13 (bl) Towlake, 15 (tr) Ffennema (b) Thomas Shanahan. NASA: 22 (bl). Shutterstock: Front cover Xpixel, back cover (tl)   (tr) Bukhta Yuri (br) Dotted Yeti, 4 (tl) BE Pictured (br) Todorean-Gabriel, 5 (br) Xpixel, 6 (bl) Kateryna Kon, 7 (tr) Kalcutta OHishiapply, 9 (tr) Suwan Wanawattanawong, 10 (tl) Dudarev Mikhail (br) Symbiot, 11 (b) Elisabeth Aardema, 12 (t) Mark Kostich, 13 (tr) Young Swee Ming, 14 (tr) Fabio Maffei (b) Sandra Standbridge, 16 (bl) Peter Altmann, 17 (cl) Lotus Images (r) Pril, 18 (t) Martin Maritz, 19 (tr) Michael Dechev (bl) Matteo Fes, 20 (tr) (bl) Slava Kovtun, 21 (t) Diyana Dimitrova (br) Bascar, 22 (c) Grisha Bruev 23 (tr) Dotted Yeti (bl) NASA images, 24 (t) Egg Head Photo (bl) Anne Powell, 25 (l) Bukhta Yurii (br) Stephen Barnes, 26 (tl) OSDG (r) Gabor Havasi, 27 (br) Wilsmedia, 28 (tc) Teerasak Ladnongkhun (b) Vchal, 29 (tc) Rawpixel.com (b) Larina Marina. 30 (bl) Sandra Standbridge, 31 (tr) Libellen87.

You can find out more about words that are underlined like **this** in the glossary on page 30.

CONTENTS

A WORLD OF YUCKY STUFF

No two people are exactly the same — even twins. We all like different things and have our own thoughts and feelings. But there are some things — yucky, slimy, squirmy, gross, smelly, and icky things — that make almost all of us say,

"EWWWW!"

Scientists think these reactions come from thousands of years ago, as humans found out how to keep safe in the world.

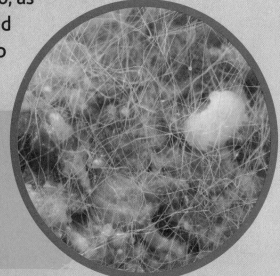

Smelly things were often full of dangerous **microbes** that could make humans ill. Squirmy things might have a poisonous bite.

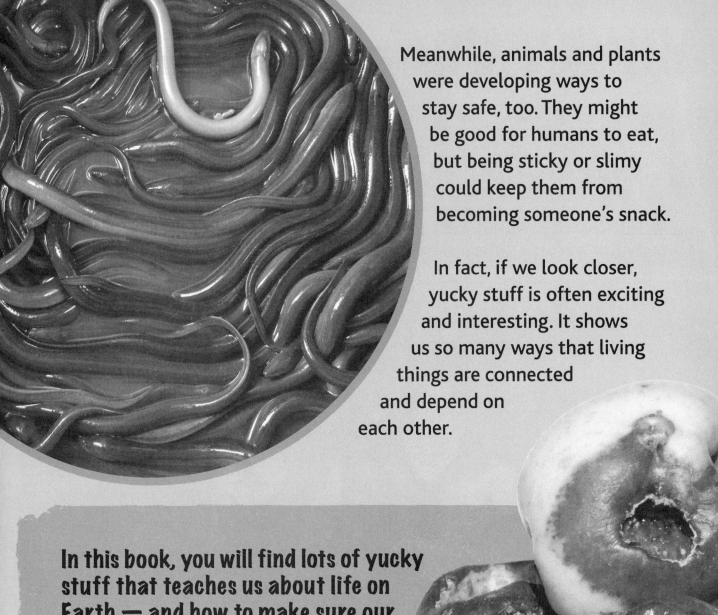

Meanwhile, animals and plants were developing ways to stay safe, too. They might be good for humans to eat, but being sticky or slimy could keep them from becoming someone's snack.

In fact, if we look closer, yucky stuff is often exciting and interesting. It shows us so many ways that living things are connected and depend on each other.

In this book, you will find lots of yucky stuff that teaches us about life on Earth — and how to make sure our planet keeps working for all living things in the future.

YUCKY US

1 **You are not 100 percent human!** Almost a quarter of the cells in your body are **bacteria** cells. But bacteria cells are much smaller than human cells, so they make up only 0.5 percent of your body mass.

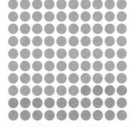

What kinds of cells are in your body

Mass of bacteria and human cells in your body

● HUMAN CELL ● BACTERIA CELL

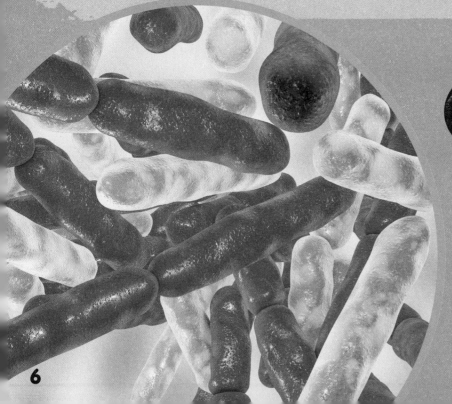

2 **Bacteria can hurt us and help us.** There are many different kinds inside us. Some can make us ill, but others can help us digest our food and help our **immune system** keep diseases away.

3 Your digestive system turns food into poop!

It is actually just a very long tube. Food goes in through your mouth. It is churned up and broken down with chemicals. Your body absorbs what you need. Anything left comes out at the end — as pee and poop.

4 Your digestive system is full of twists and turns.

In adults, food travels nearly 30 ft. (9 m).

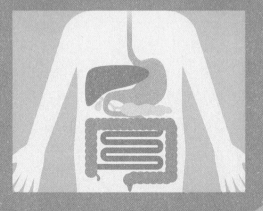

5 Tiny creatures called mites live everywhere.

Two kinds live on your face! You can only see them with a microscope. They feed on oils in your eyelashes and eyebrows!

6 **When you get hot or exercise, you sweat.**

Your skin leaks a watery liquid. This **evaporates** to keep you cool.

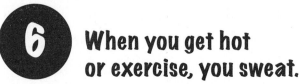

7 **A grown-up can sweat over 2.5 gallons (9.5 liters) a day.**

That's a whole bucketful!

8 **Our bodies make lots of slimy stuff** called mucus — sometimes over 2 pints (1 liter) a day! It lines all the parts of the body where air or food or even poop move in or out.

9 **Mucus lines your airways** and stops you breathing dust and other unhealthy stuff into your lungs. In your nose, it dries up and becomes boogers! They show that your nose is working the way it should.

BEASTLY FEASTS

10 **Cows are ruminants.** They swallow a lot of grass but later **regurgitate** it — bring it back into their mouths — and chew it again.

11 **Cows have four stomachs,** not just one, like us. Inside, bacteria breaks down the chewed grass, giving off gas!

12 Cows fart and burp a <u>greenhouse gas</u> called methane — about half a pound (160 grams) a day. It adds to **global warming** — causing our world to heat up.

In one day, a cow farts and burps as much gas as in 35 balloons.

13 Baby pelicans eat regurgitated food, too. They pull fish that their mother has already swallowed from her throat.

14

Many creatures are <u>cannibals</u>! That means they eat their own species. For example, female black widow spiders kept in a zoo sometimes eat their mates. In the wild, male spiders often escape.

15

Eating poop? Yuck! But some animals do. Baby elephants and hippos eat their mother's poop. Dogs, rabbits, and rats often eat their own poop. There's a good reason — it contains **nutrients** that didn't get digested the first time around.

16 **Crab spiders are cannibals from the start.** They eat their moms! The mother spider lets herself be eaten so that her babies grow strong and have a higher chance of surviving.

17 **Some animals live off other animals without killing them. They are <u>parasites</u>.** The tongue-eating louse does just that. It eats the tongue of a fish and then acts as a tongue itself, so the fish doesn't seem to mind.

18 **Starfish eat outside but it's no picnic!** They push their stomach out of their mouth and wrap it around their **<u>prey</u>**. Chemicals then digest the prey into a kind of soup, which the starfish sucks up.

SAFE IN SLIME

19 **A female frog may lay 2,000 eggs** at a time, but then she leaves them in shallow water to hatch into tadpoles and grow into frogs. The slippery jelly around each egg protects it from some **predators**.

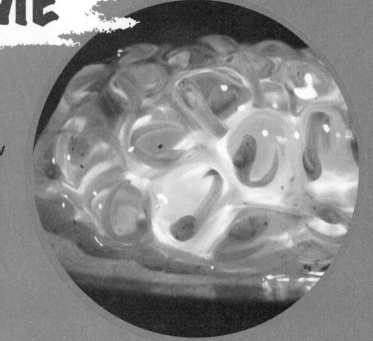

20 **Blobs of spit on stems and leaves** are often made by the young of small, sap-sucking insects called spittlebugs or froghoppers. The spit hides them from predators and keeps them moist.

21 Long slithery hagfish don't have backbones. When attacked, they make over 5 gallons (20 liters) of disgusting slime, covering their predators in goo.

22 Slugs leave a slimy footprint wherever they go, and slime may make it harder for birds to grab them. Some, like banana slugs, grow to almost 10 in. (25 cm) long.

STINKY STUFF

23 **The cat-sized skunk has a stinky weapon.** It can spray a smelly liquid from two squirters on its rear end up to 10 ft. (3 m) to keep enemies away. The smell is so strong it can cause breathlessness and even blindness.

If the wind is right, even humans can detect a skunk's smell over a mile (1.6 km) away.

24 **The world's stinkiest bug smells like rotting meat.** The shore earwig squirts out a smelly liquid so that lizards or birds that try to eat it spit it out right away!

25 The stinkiest flower in the world is also the largest.

The titan arum from Sumatra, Southeast Asia, smells of dead animals — not to keep creatures away but to attract beetles and flies that feed on **carrion**. When the insects crawl over the flower, they **pollinate** it.

26

Some say the fruit of the durian tree smells like turpentine, rotten onions, or sewage. Squirrels, orangutans, and even elephants can smell the Southeast Asian tree half a mile (0.8 km) away. They eat the fruit, wander away, and later poop out the seeds, which grow into new trees.

FUNKY POOP

27 **Dung beetles live in dung, eat dung, lay their eggs in dung, or bury dung.** They roll it into balls that can weigh 10 times more than they do. This is useful! The beetles get rid of cattle dung and make the soil richer by burying it.

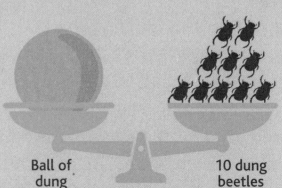

Ball of dung

10 dung beetles

28 **Parent birds often eat their nestlings' poop.** The baby birds have not digested all the worms and insects they've been given, so their parents make use of it. When the nestlings are older, the parents carry the poop away instead.

29 **Sewers are the big pipes that carry poop and wastewater away from our homes.** Too often, melted fat poured into drains gets mixed up with wet wipes and other stuff that should not be flushed and forms giant, gross **fatbergs** that block pipes. Be good to your drains!

30 **In cities, huge amounts of (mainly human) poop need to be made safe in a sewage plant.** Useful bacteria is used to get rid of harmful bacteria that might cause disease. The liquid that is left can be safely drained into rivers or spread on farmland.

ICKY, STICKY FUN

31 **Babies learn about the world by getting messy.** By finding out how things feel, smell, and taste, they learn about their own senses and explore their environment.

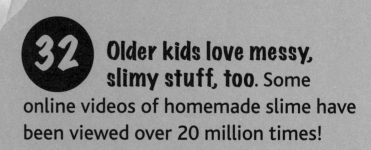

32 **Older kids love messy, slimy stuff, too.** Some online videos of homemade slime have been viewed over 20 million times!

33 Would you eat something an insect had chewed and spat out? Probably. That's how bees make honey. They collect nectar from flowers, then spit it into cells in their hives. It takes 12 bees their whole lives to make one teaspoon (5 ml) of honey.

34 Sap is a watery substance made by trees. It sometimes oozes out of the trunk in sticky drips. That sounds yucky, but some maple trees make sap that can be turned into delicious maple syrup.

STOMACH-TURNING SPACE

35 **In space, astronauts are weightless.** They float about unless they are tethered inside their spacecraft. To practice this, they fly in a plane that zooms up and down like a roller-coaster. The plane is nicknamed the "vomit comet" because one in three astronauts becomes very sick.

25 seconds of total weightlessness

20 seconds going up

20 seconds going down

36 **Astronauts drink their own sweat and pee.** It sounds gross, but these liquids are collected and processed to make them safe to drink. It's out-of-this-world recycling.

37 **In 2019, living creatures landed on the Moon.**
A spacecraft crash-landed there with eight-legged animals called tardigrades, or "water bears," on board. These tiny creatures are tough. They have been dried out, so they are not really living, but they will come alive again if they are put in water. Luckily, there's no water on the Moon — at the moment.

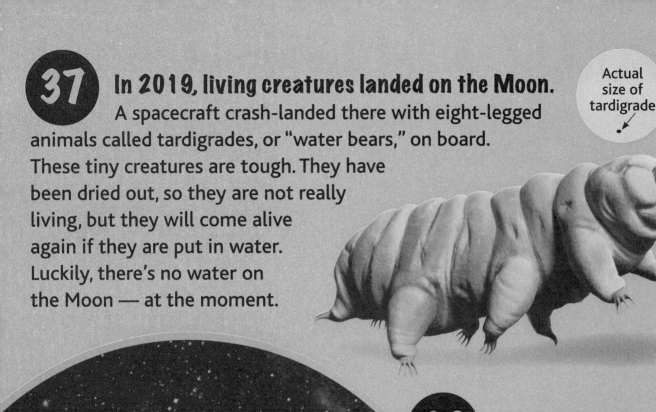

Actual size of tardigrade

38 **Earth is not the only planet in our solar system to have stinky stenches.**
Uranus smells of rotten eggs because its atmosphere contains a gas called hydrogen sulfide.

SPOILED ROTTEN

39 **Something yucky happens to food that is no longer good to eat.** Fruits like this apple soon start to **decay**. We sometimes say that food has "gone bad" but it's not really bad. It's being recycled!

40 **Microorganisms are at work in decaying plants and fruits.** Bacteria and fungi get to work to break down the plants and fruits and digest them, changing them into simpler materials. The same thing happens to animals that die, too.

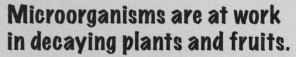

Molds are fungi — so are mushrooms. They may grow on a decaying tree trunk.

 Worms help to recycle dead plants.
They eat almost anything that was once alive, breaking it down and passing it out as rich compost.

 Other animals help, too. Scavengers eat dead animals. Their bodies use this food for energy and growing. Anything they can't use comes out as poop. Then the microorganisms get to work on that!

43 **Flies lay their eggs on decaying plants and animals.** When the eggs hatch into maggots, on their way to becoming flies, they don't need to go looking for food. It's right there!

44 **Humans have learned from what happens in nature.** Gardeners make compost from plant material and fruit and vegetable scraps. Look what gradually happens!

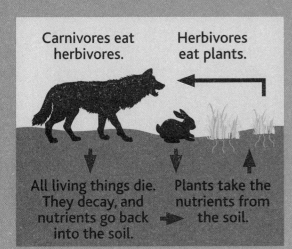

Carnivores eat herbivores.

Herbivores eat plants.

All living things die. They decay, and nutrients go back into the soil.

Plants take the nutrients from the soil.

45 Decay is a cycle — it goes around and around just like a bicycle wheel! Plants use nutrients from the soil. Herbivores eat the plants. Carnivores eat the herbivores. All living things die. Microorganisms help living things decay. Nutrients go back into the soil.

46 Would you want to grow up in a decaying home? Australian bush turkeys do! They build huge mounds of decaying leaves and lay their eggs in them. Decay heats up the mound, just like in a compost pile, and keeps the eggs warm.

WORLD OF WASTE

47 **Nature is amazing at recycling. Humans still have a lot to learn.** We each throw away a huge amount of garbage every year. Most of it goes into landfills — buried in the ground. This is hiding the yucky stuff, not dealing with it.

48 **Plastics were invented only just over a hundred years ago.** They are useful in so many ways but are very hard to get rid of. It can take over 800 years for most plastics to **biodegrade**. What seems like useful stuff is often just yucky stuff, really.

49 Plastic waste is everywhere. It is found in oceans across the world. Tiny particles, called microplastics, have even been found in snow falling in the Arctic and in sea ice.

50 To stop our whole world becoming yucky, we need to reduce, reuse, and recycle, but most of all, we need to rethink how we live in our world.

GLOSSARY

bacteria Tiny organisms that can make living things rot, help fermentation, or cause disease.

biodegrade To break down through the action of living organisms.

cannibal An animal that eats its own kind.

carrion Rotting flesh of dead animals.

decay To gradually rot or become rotten.

evaporate To turn from liquid into gas.

fatberg A large mass of fat and waste material in a sewage.

global warming An increase in the world's temperature caused by harmful (greenhouse) gases in the atmosphere.

greenhouse gas Any harmful atmospheric gas such as carbon dioxide that absorbs and emits radiant energy and contributes to global warming.

immune system All the organs and processes in the human body that protect it from illness.

microbe A very small living thing that you can see only with a microscope.

nutrients Substances that help animals and plants grow.

parasite Small animal or plant that lives on or inside a larger animal or plant and gets its food from it.

pollinate To transfer pollen from one flower to another to aid fertilization.

predator An animal that hunts and kills other animals for food.

prey The animals that a predator hunts and kills for food.

regurgitate To bring back partly digested food from the stomach to the mouth.

scavenger An animal that eats dead animals or rotten plants.

FIND OUT MORE

WEBSITES

https://www.icanteachmychild.com/ gross-science-experiments
Grow mold, make fake snot, create a blood sensory bin... all in the name of science.

https://www.homesciencetools.com
Look for the slime recipe section and have a go at making some at home!

https://www.reusethisbag.com/articles/ kids-guide-to-recycling/
It is never too early to learn how to reduce, reuse, and recycle.

PLACES TO VISIT

Disgusting Food Museum,
Los Angeles, CA

Eighty yucky delicacies from all over the world, from the smelly durian fruit to Sardinian maggot cheese.

Insectarium and Butterfly Pavilion,
Philadelphia, PA

Enjoy close encounters with a variety of multi-legged creepy crawlies before entering the colorful butterfly kingdom.

Brooklyn Children's Museum, Brooklyn, NY

With fantastic hands-on recycling exhibits to learn how to look after the planet.

BOOKS

That's Gross!: Icky Facts That Will Test Your Gross-Out Factor,
National Geographic Kids, 2012

Slimy Spawn and Other Gruesome Life Cycles (Disgusting and Dreadful Science),
Franklin Watts, 2017

Disgusting Science: A Revolting Look at What Makes Things Gross,
Macmillan Children's Books, 2014

INDEX